Thomas Shepard, John Eliot

The Clear Sunshine of the Gospel Breaking Forth Upon the Indians in New-England

Thomas Shepard, John Eliot

The Clear Sunshine of the Gospel Breaking Forth Upon the Indians in New-England

ISBN/EAN: 9783744710695

Printed in Europe, USA, Canada, Australia, Japan

Cover: Foto ©ninafisch / pixelio.de

More available books at **www.hansebooks.com**

THE

CLEAR SUNSHINE

OF THE

GOSPEL

Breaking Forth upon the Indians

IN

NEW-ENGLAND.

By THOMAS SHEPARD.

SPE ET LABORE

J S

NEW YORK:
REPRINTED FOR JOSEPH SABIN.
1865.

THE
Clear Sunſhine of the Goſpel
BREAKING FORTH
UPON THE
INDIANS
IN
NEW-ENGLAND.
OR,

An Hiſtoricall Narration of Gods
Wonderfull Workings upon ſundry of the
INDIANS, both chief Governors and Common
people, in bringing them to a willing and
deſired ſubmiſſion to the Ordinances of
the Goſpel; and framing their hearts to an
earneſt inquirie after the knowledge of
God the Father, and of Jeſus Chriſt
the Saviour of the World.

By Mr. THOMAS SHEPARD Miniſter of the Goſpel of
Jeſus Chriſt at *Cambridge* in *New-England*.

Iſaiah 2. 2, 3.   *And it ſhall come to paſſe in the laſt dayes, that the mountain of the*
Lords houſe ſhall bee eſtabliſhed in the top of the mountains, and ſhall bee exalted
above the hills ; and all Nations ſhall flow unto it.
And many people ſhall go and ſay, Come ye and let us go up to the mountain of the Lord
to the houſe of the God of Jacob, and he will teach us of his wayes, and we will walk
in his paths : for out of Zion ſhall go forth the Law, and the word of the Lord from
Jeruſalem.

London, Printed by *R. Cotes* for *Bellamy* at the three golden
Lions in *Cornhill* near the Royall Exchange, 1648.

TO THE
RIGHT HONOVRABLE
THE
LORDS & COMMONS
Aſſembled
In High Court of Parliament.

Right Honorable,

Heſe *few* ſheets *preſent* unto your view a *ſhort* but welcome *diſcourſe* of the viſitations of the *moſt High* upon the *ſaddeſt* ſpectacles of *degeneracy* upon earth, The *poore Indian* People: the *diſtance* of place, (if our *ſpirits* be right) will be no *leſſening* of the mercy, nor of our *thankefulneſſe,* That *Chriſt* is glorified, that the *Goſpel* doth any where find *footing ;* and ſucceſſe is a *mercy* as well worthy the *praiſe* of the *Saints* on Earth, as the *joy* of the *Angels* in heaven. The *report* of this mercy is *firſt* made to you, who are the *Repreſentative* of this Nation, That in you *England* might bee ſtirred up, to be

Re-

Rejoycers in, and Advancers of thefe promifing beginnings. And becaufe to You an *account* is *firft* due of the *fucceffe* of the Gofpel in thofe *darke* corners of the World, which have been fo much *enligtened* by Your favour, *enlivened* by Your refolutions, *encouraged* by Your fore-paft indeavours for God, & hope ftil being parts of Your felves, to be *further* ftrengthned by Youre benigne *afpeEts* and bountifull *influences* on them.

The prefent *troubles* have not fo far *obliterated* and worn out the fad *impreffions* which *former* times have made upon our fpirits, but we can *fadly* remember thofe *deftructive* defignes which were on foot, and carryed on for the *IntroduEtion* of fo great *evils* both into *Church and State;* In order to which it was the *endeavour* of the *Contrivers* and *Promoters* of thofe defignes, *to waft* the number of the godly, as thofe who would never be brought to *comply* in fuch deftructive enterprifes; which was attempted by *banifhing* and *forcing* fome abroad, by *burthening* and *affliEting* all at home. Among
thofe

thofe who *tafted* of the *firft*, I fay not the
worft fort of their cruelty, were thefe our
Brethren, who to enjoy the *liberties* of the
Gofpel, were *content* to fit downe, and pitch
their *tents* in the *utmoft* parts of the Earth,
hoping that there they might be out of the
reach of their malice, as they were affured
they were beyond the *bounds* of their love.
God who doth often make mans *evill* of fin,
ferviceable to the *advancement* of the *riches*
of his owne Grace; The moft *horrid* act
that ever was done by the *fonnes* of men, the
murther of Chrift, God made *ferviceable* to
the higheft *purpofes* of Grace and mercy
that ever *came* upon his breaft; That God
doth fhew that hee had *mercifull* ends, in
this their *malicious* purpofe: as hee fuffer'd
Paul to be caft into prifon, to *convert* the
Jaylor, to be fhipwrackt at *Melita*, to *preach*
to the *barbarians*, fo he *fuffer'd* their way
to be *ftopped* up here, and their perfons to be
banifhed hence, that hee might *open* a paffage
for them in the Wilderneffe, and make them
inftruments to draw foules to him, who had
been fo long *eftranged* from him.

Acts 16. 30,
33, 34.
Acts 28. 1. 11.

It

The Epiſtle

It was the end of the *adverſary* to ſup-
preſſe, but Gods to *propagate* the Goſpel;
theirs to *ſmother* and put out the light,
Gods to *communicate* and diſperſe it to the
utmoſt corners of the Earth; that as one
faith of *Paul, his blindneſſe gave light to the
whole World,* ſo we hope God will make
their diſtance and *eſtrangedneſſe* from us, a
meanes of *bringing* many near and in to ac-
quaintance with him.

ecitas *Pauli*
tius orbis il-
ninatio.
ts 9. 9.

Indeed *a long time* it was before God let
them ſee any *farther* end of their comming o-
ver, then to *preſerve* their conſciences, *cheriſh*
their Graces, *provide* for their ſuſtenance:
But when *Providences* invited their return, he
let them *know* it was for ſome farther Arrand
that hee *brought* them thither, giving them
ſome *Bunches* of Grapes, ſome *Cluſters* of Figs
in *earneſt* of the proſperous *ſucceſſe* of their
endeavours upon thoſe *poor out caſts:* The *utmoſt* ends of the earth are *deſigned* and promiſed to be *in time* the poſſeſſions of Chriſt;
And *hee ſends his Miniſters into every place
where he himſelfe intends to come,* and take poſ-
ſeſſion.

il. 2. 8.
l. 5. 10, 11,
12.
:. 11. 9, 10.
ıke 10. 1.

feffion. Where the *Miniftery* is the *Harbinger* and goes before, Chrift and *Grace* will *certainly* follow after.

This little we fee is *fomething* in hand, to *earneft* to us thofe things which are in hope; fomething in *poffeffion*, to affure us of the *reft* in promife, when the *ends* of the earth fhall fee his glory, and *the Kingdmes of the world fhall become the Kingdomes of the Lord and his Chrift, when hee fhall have Dominion from Sea to Sea, and they that dwell in the wilderneffe fhall bow before him.* And if the *dawn* of the *morning* be fo delightfull, what will the *clear* day be? If the *firft fruits* be fo precious, what wil the *whole harveft* be? if fome *beginnings* be fo ful of joy, what will it be when God fhall *perform* his *whole* work, when *the whole earth fhall be full of the knowledge of the Lord, as the waters cover the Sea,* and Eaft and Weft fhal fing together the fong of the Lamb?

Pfal. 22 27.
Rev. 11. 15.
Pfal. 72. 8, 9,
10, 11.

In *order* to this what doth God *require* of us, but that we fhould *ftrengthen* the hands, *incourage* the hearts of thofe who are at *work* for him, *conflicting* with difficulties, *wreftling* with

with difcouragements, to *fpread the* Gofpel, & in that, the *fame* and honor of this Nation, to the *utmoft* ends of the earth? It was the *defign* of your *enemies* to make them *little*, let it be your *endevor* to *make* them *great*, their *greatneffe* is your ftrength. Their enemies threatned *their* hands fhould *reach* them for evil, God *difappointed* them; And let your *hands* reach them now for good; there is enough in them to fpeak then fit *objêtes* of your incouragement, they are men of *choice* fpirits, not *frighted* with dangers, *foftned* with allurements, nor *dif-couraged* with difficulties, *preparing* the way of the Lord in thofe *unpaffable* places of the earth, dealing with fuch *whom* they are to *make* men, before they can *make* them Chrift-ians. They are fuch who are *impreffed* for your fervice in the *fervice* of Chrift, can *ftand* alone, but defire to have *dependence* on you, they feare not the *malice* of their enemies, but *de-fire* the countenance and incouragement of their friends; And fhal your *Honors* in *con-fideration* of their *former* fufferings, their *pre-*
fent

fent fervice, and *reall* defervings, *help the day of fmall things among them;* fhal you intereft them in your affiftances, as you are interefted in their affections, you wil thereby not only *further* thefe *beginnings* of God by *incouraging* their hearts, and *ftrengthning* their hands to *work* for him, but alfo (as we humbly conceive) much add to the *comfort* of your owne *accounts* in the day of the Lord, and lay greater obligations on them *yet more* to *pray* for you, to *promote* your counfels, and together with us your *unworthy fervants* to *write down* themfelves,

Yours humbly devoted in the fervice of the Gofpel.

Stephen Marfhall	*John Downam*	*Tho. Goodwin*
Jeremy Whitaker	*Philip Nye*	*Tho. Cafe*
Edm. Calamy	*Syd. Symptfon*	*Simeon Afhe*
William Greenhill	*William Carter*	*Samuel Bolton.*

TO THE

Godly and well affected of
this Kingdome of *ENGLAND*;
who pray for, and rejoyce in, the
thrivings of the Gofpel of our
LORD JESVS.

Chriftian Reader,

*I*F *ever thou hadft experience of this day of power, thefe vifitations of Chrift upon thine own fpirit; I fuppofe thee to be one who haft* embarqu'd *many prayers for the* fucceffe *of the Gofpel in thefe* darke corners *of the earth; to* ftrengthen *thy faith,* inlarge *thy heart, and affure thy foul that God is* a God hearing prayers: *An* account *is here given to thee of the* conquefts *of the Lord Iefus upon thefe poor out-cafts, who have thus long been eftranged from him, fpilt like* water *upon the ground and none to gather them.* Formerly *thou had,* The Day-break, *fome* dawnings *of light, after a long and black night of darkenes, here thou* feeft *the* fun is up, *which wee* hope *will* rejoice like the ftrong man to run its race, *fcattering thofe thick clouds of darkneffe, and* fhining *brighter and brighter* till it come to a perfect day. *Thefe few fheets give thee fome* footing *for fuch thoughts, and fome further* incouragements *to wait & pray for the* accomplifhment *of fuch things.* Here thou mayft fee, the Miniftry *is precious,* the feet of them who bring glad tidings beautifull, Ordinances *defired, the* Word *frequented*

and

and attended, the Spirit *alfo going forth in* power *and efficacy with it, in* awakening *and* humbling *of them, drawing forth thofe* affections *of forrow, and expreffions of* tears *in abundance, which no tortures or* extremities *were ever obferved to* force *from them, with* lamenting: *we read here, their leaving of finne, they* forfake *their* former *evill wayes, and fet up* fences *never to returne by making* laws *for the* punifhment *of thofe fins wherein they have lived, and to which they have been fo much addicted. They fet up* prayers *in their families* morning *and* evening, *and are in* earneft *in them; And with* more affection *they* crave *Gods bleffing upon a little parched corn, &* Indian *ftalks, then many of us do upon our greateft plenty and abundance. They* reft *on the* Lords day, *and make laws for the* obfervation *of it, wherein they* meet *together to pray & inftruct one another in the things of God, which have been* communicated *to them. They renounce their* diaboliccall *Charmes and Charmers, and many of thofe who were* practitioners *in thefe finfull and foul-undoing Arts, being made naked,* convinced *and afhamed of their evill,* forfake *their way, and betake themfelves to prayer, preferring the* Chriftian Charm, *before their* diabolical Spells: *herein God making good that promife* Zeph. 2. 11. I will famifh al the Gods of the earth, (*which he doth by withdrawing the worfhippers, and throwing contempt upon the worfhip*) And men fhal worfhip me alone every one from his place, even all the Ifles of the Heathens.

All thefe are hopefull prefages *that God is* going out *in his* power *and grace to* conquer *a people to himfelf; That he begins to caft an* owning *look on them, whom he*
hath

To the Reader.

hath so long neglected *& despised. And indeed God may wel* feek *out for other* ground *to fow the feed of his* Ordinances *upon, feeing the* ground *where it hath been* fown *hath brought forth no* better *fruit to him; he may may well* befpeak *another people to himfelf, feeing he* finds *no better* entertainment *among the people he hath* efpoufed *to him, and that by fo many* mercies, priviledges, indeerments, ingagements. *We have as many* fad fymptomes, *of a* declining, *as thefe poor outcafts have* glad prefages *of a* Rifing *Sun among them. The* Ordinances *are as much* contemned *here, as* frequented *there; the* Miniftery *as much* difcouraged *here, as* embraced *there;* Religion *as much derided, the* ways *of godlinefs as much* fcorned *here, as they can be* wifhed *and defired there; generally wee are* fick *of plenty, wee furfet of our abundance, the worft of* Surfets, *and with our* loathed Manna *and* difdained *food,* God *preparing them a* Table *in the wildernes; where our* fatieties, *wil be their* fufficiencies; *our* complaints, *their* contents; *our* burthens, *their* comforts; *if he cannot have an* England *here, he can have an* England *there; &* baptize *& adopt them into thofe* priviledges, *which wee have* looked *upon as our burthens. We have* fad decayes *upon us, we are a* revolting *Nation, a people* guilty *of great* defection *from God. Some fall from the* worfhip *of God so their old* fuperftitions, *and corrupt worfhip, faying with thofe in Ieremy,* It was better with us then now. *Some fall from the* doctrin *of grace to* errors, *fome to* damnable, *others to* defiling, *fome to* deftructive, *others to* corruptive *opinions. Some fal from* profeffed *feeming holynes, to fin & profanenes;*
who

who like blazing *comets did ſhine* bright *for a time, but after have* ſet *in a* night *of darknes. We have many* ſad ſymptomes *on us, we* decay *under all the* means *of nouriſhment, are* barren *under all* Gods ſowings, dry *under al the* dews, *droppings ſhowres of heaven, like that Country whereof* Hiſtorians *ſpeak,* where drought cauſeth dirt, and ſhowers cauſeth duſt. *And what doth God* threaten *herein, but to* remove *the* Candle-ſticks, *to take away the Goſpel, that* pretious *Goſpel, the* ſtreams *whereof have brought ſo many* ſhips *laden with bleſſings to our ſhoar, that Goſpel under the* ſhadow *whereof we have* ſate *down and been* refreſhed *theſe many years? where the* power *is loſt, God will not* long continue *the* form, *where the* heat *is gone, he wil not* long *continue the light. The* temple *did not* preſerve *the Iews when their* hearts *were the* Synagogues *of Satan, nor ſhall any* outward priviledge *hold us up, when the* inward power *is down in our ſpirits. God hath* forſaken *other* Churches *as eminent as ever* England *was : where are the* churches *of* Aſia, *once* famous *for the goſpel, for general* Councels, *now places for* Zim *and* Ochim, *their* habitation *deſolate? where are thoſe* ancient *people of the Iews who were (ſegulla micol hagnamim)* his peculiar and choſen people of al nations? *they are* ſcattered *abroad as a curſe, and their* place *knows them no more. And ſhall I tel you?* God *hath no* need *of us, he can cal them* Gnammi, *his people, who were* Lo gnammi, *not his people, and them* beloved, *who were not* beloved. *Indeed he hath* held *up us, as if he had not* known *where to have* another *people, if he ſhould* forſake *us, we have been a* Goſhen, *when others* have

Siccitas dat lutum, imbres pulverem.

To the Reader.

have been an Egypt, *a* Canaan, *when others an* Akeldama, *the* garden *of God, when others have been a wildernesse, our* fleece *hath been* wet, *when others have been* dry : *But* know, God *hath no need of us, he can* want *no people if he* pleafe *to call; If he fpeake,* all the ends Pfal. 22.27,28. of the world fhall remember and turn unto the Lord, &c. and all the kindreds of the Nations fhall worfhip 1 Efa 9. 10. before him. *If he fet up his* ftandard, to him fhal the Gentiles flock, *and* the earth fhall be full of the knowledge of the Lord, as the waters cover the fea. *It is not for* need *but for* love *that God abides with* England, *and there is nothing out of himfelfe the* incen- Amatdeus, non tive *of this love : there can be no* reafon *given why God* aliunde hoc habet, fed ipfe *fhould* fence *us, and* fuffer *other places to lye waft, that* Eft unde amat. *we fhould bee his* Garden, *and other places a* Wildernes, Aug. *that he fhould* feed *us with the* bread *of Heaven, and* fuffer *others to* ftarve, *men of the fame mould, his* off-fpring *as well as we, and fuch (did he* conquer *to him-felfe) were likely to doe him* more *fervice, bring him* more *glory then we have done. We fee fomething here done in order to fuch a work, our* Harveft *is much over, we fee little incomes, there we fee the* fields are ripe for harveft ; *here the* miniftry *is contemned,* there *the* feet of them that bring glad tydings are beautifull ; *we have* outlived *the power and efficacy of Ordinances, there God goes forth with* life *and power ; we can* outfit *the moft fpeaking and* winning difcoveries *of Chrift, there every* notion, *breeds* motion *in them ; the* glory *of the Lord is much* departed *from us, there his* rifing *is* confpicuous and glorious. *The* blind *man found it* good *to be in the* way *where Chrift came : And who would be*

in

The Epiftle

in Ægypt *when there is* light *in* Gofhen? *Oh that*
England *would be* quickned *by their rifings, and* weep
over her own declinings! What a wonder *is it that they
fhould doe* fo much, *and we* fo little, *that they fhould be*
men *in their infancy, and we fuch* children *in our*
manhood, *that they fo active, we fo dead? That which
was* Hieroms *complaint may be ours,* O that Infidelity
fhould do that which thofe who profeffe thenmfelvs

beleevers cannot do ! *We have the* light *of former
times, but want the* heat, *knowledge* abounds *as the*
waters cover *the fea, but we* want *the falt ; we have a*
form *of* Godlineffe, *but want the* power : *And it wil be*
fmal *comfort fhould God* continue *to us the form, and*
cary *to others the* power, *to fuffer us to* waft *our felves
with* unneceffary *brangles (which are the* fweat *of the
times) and in the mean to cary the life and* power *of*
Religion *unto others.*

    Let thefe poor Indians *ftand up* incentives *to us, as
the Apoftle fet up the* Gentiles *a* provocation *to the*

Iews : *who knows but God* gave *life to* New England,
to quicken Old, *and hath* warmed *them, that they
might* heat *us,* raifed *them from the dead, that they
might* recover *us from that confumption, and thofe fad*
decayes *which are come upon us ?*

    This fmal Treatife *is an* Effay *to that end, an* Indian
Sermon, *though you will not* hear *us, poffibly when fome*
rife *from the* dead *you will* hear *them. The* main
Doctrin *it preacheth unto all, is to* value *the* Gofpel,
prize *the* Miniftry, loath *not your* Manna, *furfet not
of your plenty, be* thankfull *for* mercies, fruitfull *under
means :* Awake *from your flumber,* repair *your decayes,*
                  redeem

To the Reader.

redeem *your time,* improve *the feafons of your peace;* anfwer *to cals,* open *to knocks,* attend *to whifpers,* obey *commands; you have a* name *you live, take heed you bee not* dead, *you are* Chriftians *in* fhew, *be fo* indeed: *leaft as you have* loft *the power, God take away from you the form alfo.*

And you that are Minifters *learn by this not to* defpond *though you fee not* prefent *fruit of your labors,* though you fifh all night and catch nothing. *God hath a* fullneffe *of time to* perform *all his purpofes. And the* deepeft *degeneracies, & wideft eftrangements from God, fhall be no* bar or obftacle *to the* power *and freeneffe of his owne grace when that* time *is come.*

And you that are Merchants, *take* incouragement *from hence to* fcatter *the beames of light, to* fpread *and propagate the* Gofpel *into thofe dark* corners *of the earth; whither you* traffick *you* take much *from them, if you can* carry *this to them, you wil make them an* abundant *recompence. And you that are* Chriftians *indeed, rejoice to fee the* Curtaines *of the* Tabernacle *inlarged, the* bounds *of the Sanctuary extended,* Chrift *advanced, the* Gofpel *propagated, and fouls faved. And if ever the love of God did* center *in your hearts, if ever the fenfe of his goodnefs hath begot* bowels *of compaffion in you, draw them forth* towards *them whom God hath* fingled *out to be the* objects *of his grace and mercy; lay out your prayers, lend your affiftance to carry on this* day of the Lord *begun among them. They are not able (as* Mofes *faid)* to bear the burthen of that people alone, *to make* provifion *for the* children *whom God hath given them; & therefore it is requifite the* fpiritual community

C   *fhould ſhould help to bear part with them.* Many of the young ones *are given and taken in, to be* educated *& brought up in* Schooles, *they are* naked *and muſt be* clad, *they* want *al things, and muſt be* ſupplyed. *The Parents alſo, and many others being convinced of the evill of an* idle life, *deſire to be* employed *in honeſt labor, but they* want inſtruments *and tooles to ſet them on work, and* caſt-garments *to throw upon thoſe bodies,* that their loins may bleſſe you, *whoſe* ſouls *Chriſt hath cloathed. Some* worthy perſons *have given much ; and if God ſhall* move *the heart of others to* offer willingly *towards the building of Chriſt a* Spirituall temple, *it will certainly* remain *upon their account, when the* ſmalleſt rewards *from God, ſhall be better than the greateſt layings out for God. But we are making a relation, not a collection ; we leave the whole to your Chriſtian conſideration, not doubting but they who have taſted of mercy from God, will*

Tit. 9. 14.

be ready to exerciſe compaſſion to others, & commend you unto him who gave himſelf for us, that hee might redeem us from all iniquity, and purifie *as well as purchaſe* unto himſelf a peculiar people, zealous of good works.

Stephen Marſhall	*Iohn Downam*	*Tho. Goodwin*
Ier. Whitaker	*Philip Nye*	*Tho. Caſe*
Edmund Calamy	*Sy. Simpſon*	*Simeon Aſhe*
William Greenhill	*Williamet Cart.*	*Samuel Bolton.*

THE

THE

CLEARE SVNSHINE

OF THE

GOSPELL,

Breaking forth upon the INDIANS in *New-England*.

Much Honored and deare Sir,

Hat glorious and fudden rifing of Chrift Jefus upon our poore *Indians* which began a little before you fet faile from thefe fhores, hath not beene altogether clouded fince, but rather broken out further into more light and life, wherewith the moft High hath vifited them; and becaufe fome may call in queftion the truth of the firft relation, either becaufe they may thinke it too good newes to be true, or becaufe fome perfons maligning the good of the Countrey, are apt, as to aggravate to the utmoft any evill thing againft it, fo to vilifie and extenuate any good thing in it : and becaufe your felfe defired to heare

how

how farre ſince God hath carried on that worke,
which yur owne eyes ſaw here begun; I ſhall therefore as faithfully and as briefly as I can, give you a
true relation of the progreſſe of it, which I hope may
be a ſufficient confirmation of what hath been pub-
liſhed to the world before, having this as the chiefe
end in my owne eye, that the precious Saints and
people of God in *England,* beleeving what hath been
and may bee reported to them, of theſe things, may
help forward this work together with us by their
prayers and prayſes, as we deſire to doe the like for
the worke of Chriſt begun among them there.　I
dare not ſpeake too much, nor what I thinke about
their converſion, I have ſeen ſo much falſeneſſe in
that point among many Engliſh, that I am ſlow to
beleeve herein too haſtily concerning theſe poore
naked men; onely this is evident to all honeſt hearts
that dwell neer them, and have obſerved them, that
the work of the Lord upon them (what ever it bee)
is both unexpected and wonderfull in ſo ſhort a time;
I ſhall ſet downe things as they are, and then your
ſelfe and others to whom theſe may come, may judge
as you pleaſe of them.

　　　Soon after your departure hence, the awakening
of theſe *Indians* in our Towne raiſed a great noyſe
among all the reſt round about us, eſpecially about
Concord ſide where the *Sachim* (as I remember) and
one or two more of his men, hearing of theſe things
and of the preaching of the Word, and how it wrought
among them here, came therefore hither to *Noonanetum* to the *Indian* Lecture, and what the Lord ſpake

*An inferiour Prince.

*An Indian town ſo called.

to

to his heart wee know not, only it feems hee was fo
farre affected, as that he defired to become more like
to the Englifh, and to caft off thofe *Indian* wild and
finfull courfes they formerly lived in; but when
divers of his men perceived their *Sachims* mind, they
fecretly oppofed him herein; which oppofition being
known, he therefore called together his chiefe men
about him, & made a fpeech to this effect unto them,
" *viz.* That they had no reafon at all to oppofe thofe
" courfes the Englifh were now taking for their good,
" for (faith hee) all the time you have lived after the
" *Indian* fafhion under the power and protection of
" higher *Indian Sachems*, what did they care for you?
" they onely fought their owne ends out of you, and
" therefore would exact upon you, and take away
" your fkins and your *Kettles* & your *Wampam* from
" you at their own pleafure, & this was al that they re-
" regarded: but you may evidently fee that the
" Englifh mind no fuch things, care for none of your
" goods, but onely feeke your good and welfare, and
" in ftead of taking away, are ready ·to give to you;
with many other things I now forget, which were
related by an eminent man of that town to me.
What the effect of this fpeech was, we can tell no
otherwife then as the effects fhewed it; the firft thing
was, the making of certain Lawes for their more re-
ligious and civill government and behaviour, to the
making of which they craved the affiftance of one of
the chiefe *Indians* in *Noonanetum*, a very active *Indian*
to bring in others to the knowledge of God.; defiring
withall an able faithfull man in *Concord* to record
                                                      and

* Teacher of the Church in Roxbury, that preacheth to the Indians in their own Language

and keep in writing what they had generally agreed upon.   Another effect was, their deſire of *Mr. Eliots* coming up to them, to preach, as he could find time among them ; and the laſt effect was, their deſire of having a Towne given them within the bounds of *Concord* neare unto the Engliſh.   This latter when it was propounded by the *Sachim* of the place, he was demanded why hee deſired a towne ſo neare, when as there was more roome for them up in the Country.   To which the *Sachim* replyed, that he therefore deſired it becauſe he knew that if the *Indians* dwelt far from the Engliſh, that they would not ſo much care to pray, nor would they be ſo ready to heare the Word of God, but they would be all one *Indians* ſtill ; but dwelling neare the Engliſh he hoped it might bee otherwiſe with them then.   The Town therefore was granted them ; but it ſeemes that the oppoſition made by ſome of themſelves more malignantly ſet againſt theſe courſes, hath kept them from any preſent ſetling downe : and ſurely this oppoſition is a ſpeciall finger of *Satan* refiſting theſe budding beginnings ; for what more hopefull way of doing them good then by cohabitation in ſuch Townes, neare unto good examples, and ſuch as may be continually whetting upon them, and dropping into them of the things of God ? what greater meanes at leaſt to civilize them ? as is evident in the *Cuſco* and *Mexico Indians*, more civill then any elſe in this vaſt Continent that wee know of, who were reduced by the politick principles of the two great conquering Princes of thoſe Countries after their long and tedious wars, from theſe wild and
wandring

wandring courfe of life, unto a fetling into particular
Townes and Cities: but I forbear, only to confirme
the truth of thefe things, I have fent you the orders
agreed on at *Concord* by the *Indians*, under the hand
of two faithfull witneffes, who could teftifie more, if
need were, of thefe matters: I have fent you their
owne Copy and their own hands to it, which I have
here inferted.

Conclufions and Orders made and agreed upon by divers Sachims and other principall men amongft the Indians at Concord, *in the end of the eleventh moneth, An.* 1646.

1. THat every one that fhall abufe themfelves with
   wine or ftrong liquors, fhall pay for every
   time fo abufing themfelves, 20*s.*
2. That there fhall be no more *Pawwowing* amongft
   the *Indians.* And if any fhall hereafter *Pawwow, ⁂Pawwows are
   both he that fhall *Powwow*, & he that fhall procure Witches or
   him to *Powwow*, fhall pay 20*s.* apeece. Sorcerers that
   cure by help of
3. They doe defire that they may be ftirred up to feek the devill.
   after God.
4. They defire they may underftand the wiles of Satan,
   and grow out of love with his fuggeftions, and
   temptations.
5. That they may fall upon fome better courfe to improve their time, then formerly.
6. That they may be brought to the fight of the
   finne of lying, and whofoever fhall be found faulty
   herein fhall pay for the firft offence 5 *s.* the fecond
   10*s.* the third 20*s.*

7. Whofoever

7. Whosoever shall steale any thing from another, shall restore fourfold.

8. They desire that no *Indian* hereafter shall have any more but one wife.

9. They desire to prevent falling out of *Indians* one with another, and that they may live quietly one by another.

10. That they may labour after humility and not be proud.

11. That when *Indians* doe wrong one to another, they may be lyable to censure by *fine* or the like, as the *English* are.

12. That they pay their debts to the *English*.

13. That they doe observe the Lords-Day, and whosoever shall prophane it shall pay 20 *s*.

14. That there shall not be allowance to *pick Lice,* as formerly, and eate them, and whosoever shall offend in this case shall pay for every louse a penny.

15. They will weare their *haire* comely, as the *English* do, and whosoever shall offend herein shall pay 5 *s*.

16. They intend to reforme themselves, in their former greasiing themselves, under the Penalty of 5 *s*. for every default.

A Wigwam is such a dwelling house as they live in.

17. They doe all resolve to set up prayer in their *wigwams,* and to seek to God both before and after meate.

18. If any commit the sinne of fornication, being single persons, the man shall pay 20 *s*. and the woman 10 *s*.

19. If any man lie with a beast he shall die.

20. Whosoever

20. Whofoever fhall play at their former games fhall pay 10 s.
21. Whofoever fhall commit adultery fhall be put to death.
22. Wilfull Murder fhall be punifhed with death.
23. They fhall not difguife themfelves in their mournings, as formerly, nor fhall they keep a great noyfe by howling.
24. The old Ceremony of the Maide walking alone and living apart fo many dayes 20 s.
25. No *Indian* fhall take an Englifh mans *Canooe* without leave under the penaltie of 5 s. *A Canooe is a fmall Boate.
26. No *Indian* fhall come into any *Englifh* mans houfe except he firft knock : and this they expect from the *Englifh.*
27. Whofoever beats his wife fhall pay 20 s.
28. If any *Indian* fhall fall out with, and beate another *Indian,* he fhall pay 20 s.
29. They defire they may bee a towne, and either to dwell on this fide the *Beare Swamp,* or at the Eaft fide of Mr. *Flints Pond.*

Immediately after thefe things were agreed upon, moft of the *Indians* of thefe parts, fet up Prayer morning and evening in their families, and before and after meat. They alfo generally cut their haire, and were more civill in their carriage to the *Englifh* then formerly. And they doe manifeft a great willingneffe to conform themfelves to the civill fafhions of the *Englifh.* The Lords day they keepe a day of reft, and minifter what edification they can to one another. Thefe former orders were put into this forme by

D   Captaine

Captaine *Simond Willard* of *Concord*, whom the *Indians* with unanimous conſent intreated to bee their Recorder, being very ſolicitous that what they did agree upon might be faithfully preſerved without alteration.   *Thomas Flint.   Simon Willard.*

Theſe things thus wrought in a ſhort time about *Concord* ſide, I looke upon as fruits of the miniſtery of the Word; for although their high eſteem bred lately in them, eſpecially the chief and beſt of the *Engliſh*, together with that mean eſteem many of them have of themſelves, and therefore will call themſelves ſometimes *poore Creatures*, when they ſee and heare of their great diſtance from others of the Engliſh; I ſay, although theſe things may be ſome cauſes of making theſe orders and walking in theſe courſes, yet the chiefe cauſe ſeemes to bee the power of the Word, which hath been the chiefe cauſe of theſe Orders, and therefore it is that untill now of late they never ſo much as thought of any of theſe things.

I am not able to acquaint you very much from my owne eye and eare witneſſe of things, for you know the neare relation between me and the fire ſide uſually all winter time, onely I ſhall impart two or three things more of what I have heard and ſeen, and the reſt I ſhall relate to you as I have received from faithfull witneſſes, who teſtifie nothing to me by their writings, but what is ſeene in the open Sun, and done in the view of all the world, and generally known to be true of people abiding in theſe parts wee live in.   As

As foone as ever the fierceneffe of the winter was paft, March. 3. 1647. I went out to *Noonanetum* to the *Indian* Lecture, where Mr. *Wilfon*, Mr. *Allen*, of *Dedham*, Mr. *Dunfter*, befide many other Chriftians were prefent; on which day perceiving divers of the *Indian* women well affected, and confidering that their foules might ftand in need of anfwer to their fcruples as well as the mens; & yet becaufe we knew how unfit it was for women fo much as to afke queftions publiquely immediatly by themfelves; wee did therefore defire them to propound any queftions they would bee refolved about by firft acquainting either their Hufbands, or the Interpreter privately therewith: whereupon we heard two queftions thus orderly propounded; which becaufe they are the firft that ever were propounded by *Indian* women in fuch an ordinance that ever wee heard of, and becaufe they may bee otherwife ufefull, I fhall therefore fet them downe.

The firft queftion was propounded by the wife of one *Wampooas* a well affected *Indian, viz.* "Whether " (faid fhe) do I pray when my hufband prayes if I " fpeak nothing as he doth, yet if I like what he faith, " and my heart goes with it? (for the *Indians* will many times pray with their wives, and with their children alfo fometime in the fields) fhee therefore fearing left prayer fhould onely be an externall action of the lips, enquired if it might not be alfo an inward action of the heart, if fhe liked of what he faid.

The fecond queftion was propounded by the Wife of one *Totherfwampe*, her meaning in her queftion

(as

(as wee all perceived) was this, *viz.* " Whether a huf-
" band fhould do well to pray with his wife, and yet
" continue in his paffions, & be angry with his wife?
But the modefty and wifdome of the woman directed
her to doe three things in one, for thus fhee fpake to
us, *viz.* " Before my hufband did pray hee was much
" angry and froward, but fince hee hath begun to
" pray hee was not angry fo much, but little angry:
wherein firft fhee gave an honorable teftimony of her
hufband and commended him for the abatement of
his paffion; fecondly, fhee gave implicitly a fecret
reproofe for what was paft, and for fomewhat at prefent that was amiffe; and thirdly, it was intended by
her as a queftion whether her hufband fhould pray
to God, and yet continue in fome unruly paffions;
but fhe wifely avoyded that, left it might reflect too
much upon him, although wee defired her to expreffe
if that was not her meaning.

At this time (befide thefe queftions) there were
fundry others propounded of very good ufe, in all
which we faw the Lord Jefus leading them to make
narrow inquiries into the things of God, that fo they
might fee the reality of them. I have heard few
Chriftians when they begin to looke toward God,
make more fearching queftions that they might fee
things really, and not onely have a notion of them:
I forbeare to mention any of them, becaufe I forget
the chiefe of them; onely this wee tooke notice of
at this dayes meeting, that there was an aged *Indian*
who propofed his complaint in propounding his
queftion concerning an unruly difobedient fon, and
" what

· " what one fhould do with him in cafe of obftinacy
" and difobedience, and that will not heare Gods
" Word, though his Father command him, nor will
" not forfake his drunkenneffe, though his father
" forbid him? Unto which there were many anfwers to fet forth the finne of difobedience to parents; which were the more quickned and fharpned
becaufe wee knew that this rebellious fonne whom
the old man meant, was by Gods providence prefent
at this Lecture: Mr. *Wilfon* was much inlarged, and
fpake fo terribly, yet fo gracioufly as might have affected a heart not quite fhut up, which this young
defperado hearing (who well underftood the *Englifh*
tongue) inftead of humbling himfelf before the Lords
Word, which touched his confcience and condition
fo neare, hee was filled with a fpirit of Satan, and as
foone as ever Mr. *Wilfons* fpeech was ended hee brake
out into a loud contemptuous expreffion; *So,* faith he:
which we paffed by without fpeaking againe, leaving
the Word with him, which we knew would one day
take its effect one way or other upon him.

The latter end of this yeare Mr. *Wilfon,* Mr. *Eliot,*
and my felfe were fent for by thofe in *Yarmouth* to
meet with fome other Elders of *Plimouth pattent,* to
heare and heale (if it were the will of Chrift) the
difference and fad breaches which have been too long
a time among them, wherein the Lord was very mercifull to us and them in binding them up beyond our
thoughts in a very fhort time, in giving not only that
bruifed Church but the whole Towne alfo a hopefull
beginning of fetled peace and future quietneffe; but
Mr.

Mr. *Eliot* as hee takes all other advantages of time, ſo
hee tooke this, of ſpeaking with, and preaching to the
poore *Indians* in theſe remote places about *Cape Cod:*
in which journey I ſhall acquaint you with what all
of us obſerved.

Wee firſt found theſe *Indians* (not very farre from
ours) to underſtand (but with much difficulty) the
uſuall language of thoſe in our parts, partly in regard
to the different dialeɛt which generally varies in 40.
or 60. miles, and partly and eſpecially in regard of
their not being accuſtomed unto ſacred language
about the holy things of God, wherein Mr. *Eliot* ex-
cells any other of the *Engliſh*, that in the *Indian* language about common matters excell him : I ſay therefore although they did with much difficulty underſtand him, yet they did underſtand him, although by
many circumlocutions and variations of ſpeech and
the helpe of one or two Interpreters which were then
preſent.

Secondly, wee obſerved much oppoſition againſt
him, and hearing of him at the day appointed, eſpecially by one of the chiefeſt *Sachims* in thoſe parts, a
man of a fierce, ſtrong and furious ſpirit whom the
Engliſh therefore call by the name *Jehu:* who although
before the day appointed for preaching, promiſed
very faire that he would come and bring his men
with him ; yet that very morning when they were to
bee preſent, he ſends out almoſt all his men to Sea,
pretending fiſhing, and therefore although at laſt he
came late himſelfe to the Sermon, yet his men were
abſent, and when he came himſelf, would not ſeem

to

to underftand any thing, although hee did underftand
as fome of the *Indians* themfelves then told us, when
Mr. *Eliot* by himfelf and by them inquired of him if
he underftood what was fpoken : yet he continued
hearing what was faid with a dogged looke and dif-
contented countenance.

Thirdly, notwithftanding this oppofition wee found
another *Sachim* then prefent willing to learne, and
divers of his men attentive and knowing what was faid :
and in the time which is ufually fet apart for propounding queftions, an aged *Indian* told us openly, " That
" thefe very things which Mr. *Eliot* had taught them
" as the Commandements of God, and concerning
" God, and the making of the world by one God,
" that they had heard fome old men who were now
" dead, to fay the fame things, fince whofe death there
" hath been no remembrance or knowledge of them
" among the *Indians* untill now they heare of them
againe. Which when I heard folemnly fpoken, I
could not tell how thofe old *Indians* fhould attaine
to fuch knowledge, unleleffe perhaps by means of the
French Preacher caft upon thofe coafts many yeers
fince, by whofe miniftry they might poffibly reape
and retaine fome knowledge of thofe things ; this alfo
I hear by a godly and able Chriftian who hath much
converfe with them ; that many of them have this
apprehenfion now ftirring among them, *viz.* " That
" their forefathers did know God, but that after this,
" they fell into a great fleep, and when they did awaken
" they quite forgot him, (for under fuch metaphori-
call language they ufually expreffe what eminent
 things

things they meane:) ſo that it may ſeeme to be the
day of the Lords gracious viſitation of theſe poore
Natives, which is juſt as it is with all other people,
when they are moſt low, the wheele then turnes,
and the Lord remembers to have mercy.

Fourthly, a fourth and laſt obſervation wee took,
was the ſtory of an *Indian* in thoſe parts, telling us
of his dreame many yeers ſince, which he told us of
openly before many witneſſes when we ſate at meat:
the dreame is this, hee ſaid " That about two yeers
" before the *Engliſh* came over into thoſe parts there
" was a great mortality among the *Indians*, and one
" night he could not ſleep above half the night, after
" which hee fell into a dream, in which he did think
" he ſaw a great many men come to thoſe parts in
" cloths, juſt as the *Engliſh* now are apparelled, and
" among them there aroſe up a man all in black, with a
" thing in his hand which hee now ſees was all one
" *Engliſh* mans book ; this black man he ſaid ſtood
" upon a higher place then all the reſt, and on the one
" ſide of him were the *Engliſh*, on the other a great
" number of *Indians :* this man told all the *Indians*
" that God was *mooſquantum* or angry with them, and
" that he would kill them for their ſinnes, whereupon
" he ſaid himſelf ſtood up, and deſired to know of the
" black man what God would do with him and his
" *Squaw* and *Papooſes,* but the black man would not
" anſwer him a firſt time, nor yet a ſecond time, un-
" till he deſired the third time, and then he ſmil'd
" upon him, and told him that he and his *Papooſes*
" ſhould be ſafe, and that God would give unto them
                                                    " *Mitcheu,*

" *Mitcheu*, (*i. e.*) victualls and other good things, and fo hee awakened. What fimilitude this dream hath with the truth accomplifhed, you may eafily fee. I attribute little to dreams, yet God may fpeak to fuch by them rather then to thofe who have a more fure Word to direct and warn them, yet this dream made us think furely this *Indian* will regard the black man now come among them rather then any others of them : but whether Satan, or fear, and guilt, or world prevailed, we cannot fay, but this is certaine, that he withdrew from the Sermon, and although hee came at the latter end of it, as hoping it had been done, yet we could not perfwade him then to ftay and hear, but away he flung, and we faw him no more till next day.

From this third of *March* untill the latter end of this Summer I could not be prefent at the *Indian* Lectures, but when I came this laft time, I marvailed to fee fo many *Indian* men, women and children in *Englifh* apparell, they being at *Noonanetum* generally clad, efpecially upon Lecture dayes, which they have got partly by gift from the *Englifh*, and partly by their own labours, by which fome of them have very handfomely apparelled themfelves, & you would fcarce know them from *Englifh* people. There is one thing more which I would acquaint you with, which hapned this Summer, *viz. June* 9. the firft day of the Synods meeting at *Cambridge*, where the forenoon was fpent in hearing a Sermon preached by one of the *Elders* as a preparative to the worke of the Synod, the afternoon was fpent in hearing an *Indian* Lecture

E   where

where there was a great confluence of *Indians* all parts
to heare Mr. *Eliot*, which we conceived not unfeafon-
able at fuch a time, partly that the reports of Gods
worke begun among them, might be feen and be-
leeved of the chief who were then fent and met from
all the Churches of Chrift in the Countrey, who
could hardly beleeve the reports they had received
concerning thefe new ftirs among the *Indians*, and
partly hereby to raife up a greater fpirit of prayer for
the carrying on of the work begun upon the *Indians*,
among all the Churches and fervants of the Lord
Jefus : The Sermon was fpent in fhewing them their
miferable condition without Chrift, out of *Ephef.* 2. 1.
that they were dead in trefpaffes and finnes, and in
pointing unto them the Lord Jefus, who onely could
quicken them.

When the Sermon was done, there was a conve-
nient fpace of time fpent in hearing thofe queftions
which the *Indians* publikely propounded, and in
giving anfwers to them; one queftion was, *What
Countrey man Chrift was, and where was he born?*

Another was, *How farre off that place was from us
here?*

Another was, *Where Chrift now was?*

And another, *How they might lay hold on him, and
where, being now abfent from them?* with fome other
to this purpofe; which received full anfwers from
feverall hands. But that which I note is this, that
their gracious attention to the Word, the affections
and mournings of fome of them under it, their fober
propounding of divers fpirituall queftions, their apt-

neffe

neffe to underftand and beleeve what was replyed to
them, the readineffe of divers poore naked children
to anfwer openly the chief queftions in Catechifm
which were formerly taught them, and fuch like appearances of a great change upon them, did marvel-
loufly affect all the wife and godly Minifters, Magiftrates, & people, and did raife their hearts up to great
thankfulneffe to God ; very many deeply and abundantly mourning for joy to fee fuch a bleffed day, and
the Lord Jefus fo much known and fpoken of among
fuch as never heard of him before : So that if any in
England doubt of the truth of what was formerly
writ, or if any malignant eye fhall queftion and vilifie
this work, they will now fpeak too late, for what
was here done at *Cambridge* was not fet under a
Bufhell, but in the open Sunne, that what *Thomas*
would not beleeve by the reports of others, he might
be forced to beleeve, by feeing with his own eyes and
feeling Chrift Jefus thus rifen among them with his
own hands.

I have done with what I have obferved my felf ; I
fhall therefore proceed to give you a true relation of
what I have heard from others, and many faithfull
witneffes have feene : and firft I fhall fpeake a little
more of the old man who is mentioned in the ftory
now in print ; this old man hath much affection
ftirred up by the Word, and comming to Mr. *Eliots*
houfe (for of him I had this ftory) Mr. *Eliot* told him
that becaufe he brought his wife & all his children
conftantly to the Lecture, that he would therefore
beftow fome Cloths upon him, (it being now winter
&

& the old man naked :) which promiſe he not certainly underſtanding the meaning of, aſked therefore
of another *Indian* (who is Mr. *Eliots* ſervant and very
hopefull) what it was that Mr. *Eliot* promiſed him ?
he told him that hee ſaid hee would give him ſome
Cloths ; which when hee underſtood, hee affectionately brake out into theſe expreſſions, *God I ſee is
mercifull :* a bleſſed, becauſe a plain hearted affectionate ſpeech, and worthy *Engliſh* mens thoughts when
they put on their Cloths ; to thinke that a poor
blind *Indian* that ſcarce ever heard of God before,
that he ſhould ſee not only God in his Cloths, but
mercy alſo in a promiſe of a caſt off worne ſute of
Cloths, which were then given him, and which now
he daily weares.   But to proceed ;

  This ſame old man (as I think a little before hee
had theſe Cloths) after an *Indian* Lecture, when they
uſually come to propound queſtions ; inſtead of aſking a queſtion, began to ſpeak to the reſt of the *Indians,* and brake out into many expreſſions of won-
dring at Gods goodneſſe unto them, that the Lord
ſhould at laſt look upon them and ſend his Word as
a light unto them that had been in darkneſſe and ſuch
groſſe ignorance ſo long ; me wonder (ſaith he) at
God that he ſhould thus deale with us.   This ſpeech
expreſſed in many words in the *Indian* Language, and
with ſtrong actings of his eyes and hands, being in-
terpreted afterward to the *Engliſh,* did much alſo affect
all of them that were preſent at this Lecture alſo.

  There were this winter many other queſtions propounded, which were writ down by Mr. *Edward
                                             Jackſon*

Jackson one of our Town, conftantly prefent at thefe Lectures, to take notes both of the queftions made by the *Indians* and returned by Mr. *Eliot* to them; this man having fent me in his notes, I fhall fend you a taft of fome of them.

1 *Why fome men were fo bad, that they hate thofe men that would teach them good things?*

2 *Whether the devill or man were made firft?*

3 *Whether if a father prayes to God to teach his fons to know him, and he doth teach them himfelf and they will not learn to know God, what fhould fuch fathers doe?* (this was propounded by an old man that had rude children.)

4 A **Squaw* propounded this queftion, *Whether* *Indian wo-*fhe might not go & pray in fome private place in the* man. *woods, when her hufband was not at home, becaufe fhe was afhamed to pray in the Wigwam before company?*

5 *How may one know wicked men, who are good and who are bad?*

6 *To what Nation Jefus Chrift came firft unto, and when?*

7 *If a man fhould be inclofed in Iron a foot thick and thrown into the fire, what would become of his foule, whether could the foule come forth thence or not?*

8 *Why did not God give all men good hearts that they might bee good?*

9 *If one fhould be taken among ftrange Indians that know not God, and they would make him to fight againft fome that he fhould not, and he refufe, and for his refufall they kill him, what would become of his foule in fuch a cafe?*

They hold caſe ? This was propounded by a *ſtout fellow who
that all their was affected.
ſtout and val-
iant men have   10 *How long it is before men beleeve that have the*
a reward after *Word of God made known to them?*
death.
                  11 *How they ſhould know when their faith is good,
and their prayers good prayers?*

                  12 *Why did not God kill the Devill that made all
men ſo bad, God having all power?*

                  13 *If we be made weak by ſinne in our hearts, how
can we come before God to ſanctifie a Sabbath?*

There were many more queſtions of this kind, as
alſo many Philoſophicall about the Sunne, Moon,
Stars, Earth and Seas, Thunder, Lightning, Earth-
quakes, &c. which I forbear to make mention of, leſt
I ſhould clog your time with reading, together with
the various anſwers to them : by theſe you may perceive in what ſtreame their minds are carried, and
that the Lord Jeſus hath at laſt an enquiring people
among theſe poor naked men, that formerly never ſo
much as thought of him ; which queſtionings and
enquiries are accounted of by ſome as part of the
whitenings of the harveſt toward, wherever they are
found among any people, the good and benefit that
comes to them hereby is and will be exceeding great.

We had this year a malignant drunken *Indian*, that
(to caſt ſome reproach, as wee feared, upon this way)
boldly propounded this queſtion, Mr. *Eliot* (ſaid he)
Who made Sack? who made Sack? but he was ſoon
*That is a ſnib'd by the other *Indians*, calling it *a *Papooſe* queſ-
childiſh queſ-tion, and ſeriouſly and gravely anſwered (not ſo much
tion.
                  to his queſtion as to his ſpirit) by Mr. *Eliot*, which
                                                                  hath

hath cooled his boldneſſe ever ſince, while others
have gone on comfortably in this profitable and plea-
ſant way.

The man who ſent me theſe and the like queſtions
with their ſeverall anſwers in writing, concluded his
letter with this ſtory, which I ſhall here inſert, that
you may ſee the more of God among theſe poore
people: "Upon the 25. of *Aprill* laſt (ſaith he)
" I had ſome occaſion to go to ſpeak with *Wahun   *An Indian
" about Sun-riſing in the morning, and ſtaying ſome Sachim.
" half an hours time, as I came back by one of
" the *Wigwams*, the man of that *Wigwam* was at
" prayer; at which I was ſo much affected, that I
" could not but ſtand under a Tree within hearing,
" though I could not underſtand but little of his
" words, and conſider that God was fulfilling his
" Word, *viz. The ends of the earth ſhall remember*
" *themſelves and turne unto him;* and that Scripture,
" *Thou art the God that heareſt prayer, vnto thee ſhall*
" *all fleſh come.*
"   Alſo this preſent *September* I have obſerved one of
" them to call his children to him from their gather-
" ing of Corne in the field, and to crave a bleſſing, with
" much affection, having but a homely dinner to eate.

Theſe things me thinkes ſhould move bowels, and
awaken *Engliſh* hearts to be thankfull, it is no ſmall
part of Religion to awaken with God in family
prayer, (as it ſeemes theſe doe it early) and to crave a
bleſſing with affectionate hearts upon a homely dinner, perhaps parcht Corne or *Indian* ſtalks: I wiſh
the like hearts and wayes were ſeen in many *Engliſh*
                                                    who

who profeſſe themſelves Chriſtians, and that herein
and many the like excellencies they were become
Indians, excepting that name, as he did in another
caſe, except his bonds : and that you may ſee not only
how farre Religion, but civility hath taken place
among them, you may be pleaſed therefore to peruſe
this Court Order, which is here inſerted.

The Order made laſt Generall Court at Boſton *the* 26. *of*
May, 1647. *concerning the* Indians, &c.

VPon information that the *Indians* dwelling among
us, and ſubmitted to our government, being by
the Miniſtry of the Word brought to ſome civility,
are deſirous to have a courſe of ordinary Judicature
ſet up among them : It is therefore ordered by au-
thority of this Court, that ſome one or more of the
Magiſtrates, as they ſhall agree amongſt themſelves,
ſhall once every quarter keep a Court at ſuch place,
where the *Indians* ordinarily aſſemble to hear the
Word of God, and may then hear and determine all
cauſes both civill and criminall, not being capitall,
concerning the *Indians* only, and that the *Indian
Sachims* ſhall have libertie to take order in the nature
of Summons or Attachments, to bring any of their
own people to the ſaid Courts, and to keep a Court
of themſelves, every moneth if they ſee occaſion, to
determine ſmall cauſes of a civill nature, and ſuch
ſmaller criminall cauſes as the ſaid Magiſtrates ſhall
referre

referre to them ; and the faid *Sachims* fhall appoint
Officers to ferve Warrants, and to execute the Orders
and Judgements of either of the faid Courts, which
Officers fhall from time to time bee allowed by the
faid Magiftrates in the quarter Courts or by the Gov-
ernour : And that all fines to bee impofed upon any
Indian in any of the faid Courts, fhall goe and bee
beftowed towards the building of fome meeting
houfes, for education of their poorer children in learn-
ing, or other publick ufe, by the advice of the faid
Magiftrates and of Mafter *Eliot*, or of fuch other
Elder, as fhall ordinarily inftruct them in the true
Religion. And it is the defire of this Court, that
thefe Magiftrates and Mr. *Eliot* or fuch other Elders
as fhall attend the keeping of the faid Courts will
carefully indeavour to make the Indians underftand
our moft ufefull Lawes, and the principles of reafon,
juftice and equity whereupon they are grounded, &
it is defired that fome care may be taken of the *Indians*
on the Lords dayes.

Thus having had a defire to acquaint you with
thefe proceedings among the *Indians*, and being defirous that you might more fully underftand, efpecially from him who is beft able to judge, I did
therefore intreat my brother *Eliot* after fome conference about thefe things, to fet down under his own
hand what he hath obferved lately among them :
which I do therefore herein fend unto you in his owne
hand writing as he fent it unto mee, which I think is
worthy all Chriftian thankfull eares to heare, and

F wherein

wherein they may fee a little of the Spirit of this man of God, whom in other refpects, but efpecially for his unweariedneffe in this work of God, going up and down among them and doing them good, I think we can never love nor honour enough.

The Letter of Mr. Eliot *to* T. S. *concerning the late work of God among the* Indians.

Deare Brother,

AT your defire I have wrote a few things touching the *Indians* which at prefent came to my mind, as being fome of thofe paffages which took principall impreffion in my heart, wherein I thought I faw the Lord, and faid the finger of God is here.

That which I firft aymed at was to declare & deliver unto them the Law of God, to civilize them, wch courfe the Lord took by *Mofes*, to give the Law to that rude company becaufe of tranfgreffion, *Gal.* 3. 19. to convince, bridle, reftrain, and civilize them, and alfo to humble them. But when I firft attempted it, they gave no heed unto it, but were weary, and rather defpifed what I faid. Awhile after God ftirred up in fome of them a defire to come into the *Englifh* fafhions, and live after their manner, but knew not how to attain unto it, yea defpaired that ever it fhould come to paffe in their dayes, but thought that in 40. yeers more, fome *Indians* would be all one Englifh, and in an hundred yeers, all *Indians* here about, would fo bee: which when I heard (for fome

of

of them told me they thought fo, and that fome wife *Indians* faid fo) my heart moved within mee, abhorring that wee fhould fit ftill and let that work alone, and hoping that this motion in them was of the Lord, and that this mind in them was a preparative to imbrace the Law and Word of God; and therefore I told them that they and wee were already all one fave in two things, which make the only difference betwixt them and us: Firft, we know, ferve, and pray unto God, and they doe not: Secondly, we labour and work in building, planting, clothing our felves, &c. and they doe not: and would they but doe as wee doe in thefe things, they would be all one with *Englifh* men: they faid they did not know God, and therefore could not tell how to pray to him, nor ferve him. I told them if they would learn to know God, I would teach them: unto which they being very willing, I then taught them (as I fundry times had indeavored afore) but never found them fo forward, attentive and defirous to learn till this time, and then I told them I would come to their *Wigwams*, and teach them, their wives and children, which they feemed very glad of; and from that day forward I have not failed to doe that poore little which you know I doe.

I firft began with the *Indians* of *Noonanetum*, as you know; thofe of *Dorchefter mill* not regarding any fuch thing: but the better fort of them perceiving how acceptable this was to the Englifh, both to Magiftrates, and all the good people, it pleafed God to ftep in and bow their hearts to defire to be taught
to

to know God, and pray unto him likewiſe, and had
I not gone unto them alſo, and taught them when I
did, they had prevented me, and deſired me ſo to do,
as I afterward heard.

The effect of the Word which appears among
them, and the change that is among them is this:
Firſt, they have utterly forſaken all their *Powwaws,*
and given over that diabolicall exerciſe, being convinced that it is quite contrary to praying unto God;
yea ſundry of their *Powwaws* have renounced their
wicked imployment, have condemned it as evill, and
reſolved never to uſe it any more; others of them,
ſeeing their imployment and gaines were utterly gone
here, have fled to other places, where they are ſtill
entertained, and have raiſed lies, ſlanders, and an evill
report upon thoſe that heare the Word, and pray unto
God, and alſo upon the Engliſh that indeavour to
reclaime them and inſtruct them, that ſo they might
diſcourage others from praying unto God, for that
they account as a principall ſigne of a good man, and
call all religion by that name, praying to God; and
beſide they mock and ſcoffe at thoſe *Indians* which
pray, and blaſpheme God when they pray; as this is
one inſtance. A ſober *Indian* going up into the
countrey with two of his ſons, did pray (as his manner was at home) and talked to them of God and
Jeſus Chriſt: but they mocked, & called one of his
ſons *Jehovah,* and the other *Jeſus Chriſt:* ſo that they
are not without oppoſition raiſed by the *Powwaws,*
and other wicked *Indians.*

Againe as they have forſaken their former Religion,

gion, and manner of worſhip, ſo they doe pray unto
God conſtantly in their families, morning and evening, and that with great affeƈtion, as hath been ſeen
and heard by ſundry that have gone to their *Wigwams*
at ſuch times ; as alſo when they goe to meat they
ſolemnly pray and give thanks to God, as they ſee the
Engliſh to doe: ſo that that curſe which God threat-
ens to poure out upon the families that call not on his
name, is through his grace, and tender mercy ſtayed
from breaking forth againſt them, and when they
come to Engliſh houſes, they deſire to be taught ;
and if meat bee given them, they pray and give thanks
to God : and uſually expreſſe their great joy, that
they are taught to know God, and their great affection to them that teach them.

Furthermore they are carefull to inſtruƈt their
children, that ſo when I come they might be ready
to anſwer their Catechize, which by the often repeat-
ing of it to the children, the men and women can
readily anſwer to.

Likewiſe they are carefull to ſanƈtifie the Sabbath,
but at firſt they could not tell how to doe it, and they
aſked of mee how they ſhould doe it, propounding it
as a queſtion whether they ſhould come to the Engliſh meetings or meet among themſelves ; they ſaid,
if they come to the Engliſh meetings they underſtand
nothing, or to no purpoſe, and if they met together
among themſelves, they had none that could teach
them. I told them that it was not pleaſing to God,
nor profitable to themſelves, to hear and underſtand
nothing, nor having any that could interpret to
                                                  them.

them. Therefore I counfelled them to meet together, and defire thofe that were the wifeft and beft
men to pray, and then to teach the reft fuch things
as I had taught them from Gods Word, as well as
they could; and when one hath done, then let another
do the like, and then a third, and when that was
done afke queftions, and if they could not anfwer
them, then remember to afke me, &c. and to pray
unto God to help them therein : and this is the manner how they fpend their Sabbaths.

They are alfo ftrict againft any prophanation of
the Sabbath, by working, fifhing, hunting, &c. and
have a Law to punifh fuch as are delinquents therein
by a fine of 10*s*. and fundry cafes they have had,
wherein they have very ftrictly profecuted fuch as
have any way prophaned the Sabbath. As for example, upon a Sabbath morning *Cutchamaquin* the
Sachim his wife going to fetch water met with other
women, and fhe began to talk of worldly matters,
and fo held on their difcourfe a while, which evill
came to *Nahantons* eare, who was to teach that day
(this *Nahanton* is a fober good man, and a true friend
to the Englifh ever fince our comming) fo he bent his
difcourfe to fhew the fanctification of the Sabbath, &
reproved fuch evils as did violate the fame ; & among
other things worldly talk, and thereupon reproved
that which he heard of that morning. After hee
had done, they fell to difcourfe about it, and fpent
much time therein, hee ftanding to prove that it was
a finne, and fhe doubting of it, feeing it was early in
the morning, and in private ; and alledging that he
was

was more to blame then fhe, becaufe he had occa-
fioned fo much difcourfe in the publick meeting:
but in conclufion they determined to refer the cafe
to me, and accordingly they did come to my houfe
on the fecond day morning and opened all the matter,
and I gave them fuch directions as the Lord directed
me unto, according to his holy Word.

Another cafe was this, upon a Lords day towards
night two ftrangers came to *Wahans Wigwam* (it being ufuall with them to travaile on that day, as on
any other; (and when they came in, they told him
that at a place about a mile off they had chafed a
Rackoone, and he betook himfelf into an hollow tree,
and if they would goe with them, they might fell
the tree and take him: at which tidings, *Wahan* being willing to be fo well provided to entertain thofe
ftrangers (a common practife among them, freely to
entertain travailers and ftrangers) he fent his two fervants with them, who felled the tree, and took the
beaft. But this act of his was an offence to the reft,
who judged it a violation of the Sabbath, and moved
agitation among them: but the conclufion was, it
it was to bee moved as a queftion upon the next
Lecture day; which was accordingly done, and received fuch anfwer as the Lord guided unto by his
Word.

Another cafe was this, upon a Lords day their
publick meeting holding long, and fomewhat late,
when they came at home, in one *Wigwam* the fire was
almoft out, and therefore the man of the houfe, as he
fate by the fire fide took his Hatchet and fplit a little
dry

dry peece of wood, which they referve on purpofe
for fuch ufe, and fo kindled his fire, which being
taken notice of, it was thought to bee fuch a worke
as might not lawfully be done upon the Sabbath day,
and therefore the cafe was propounded the Lecture
following for their better information.

Thefe inftances may ferve to fhew their care of the
externall obfervation of the Sabbath day.

In my exercife among them (as you know) wee
attend foure things, befides prayer unto God, for his
prefence and blefing upon all we doe.

Firft, I catechize the children and youth; wherein
fome are very ready & expert, they can readily fay all
the Commandements, fo far as I have communicated
them, and all other principles about the creation, the
fall, the redemption by Chrift, &c. wherein alfo the
aged people are pretty expert, by the frequent repe-
tition thereof to the children, and are able to teach it
to their children at home, and do fo.

Secondly, I Preach unto them out of fome texts of
Scripture, wherein I ftudy all plainneffe, and brevity,
unto which many are very attentive.

Thirdly, if there be any occafion, we in the next
place go to admonition and cenfure; unto which they
fubmit themfelves reverently, and obediently, and
fome of them penitently confeffing their fins with
much plainneffe, and without fhiftings, and excufes:
I will inftance in two or three particulars; this was
one cafe, a man named *Wampoowas*, being in a paffion
upon fome light occafion did beat his wife, which
was a very great offence among them now (though

in

in former times it was very ufuall) and they had made
a Law againſt it, and fet a fine upon it; whereupon
he was publikly brought forth before the Affembly,
which was great that day, for our Governor and
many other Engliſh were then prefent: the man
wholly condemned himfelf without any excufe: and
when he was aſked what provocation his wife gave
him ? he did not in the leaſt meafure blame her but
himfelf, and when the quality of the finne was opened, that it was cruelty to his own body, and againſt
Gods Commandement, and that paffion was a finne,
and much aggravated by fuch effeĉts, yet God was
ready to pardon it in Chriſt, &c. he turned his face
to the wall and wept, though with modeſt indeavor
to hide it; and fuch was the modeſt, penitent, and
melting behavior of the man, that it much affeĉted
all to fee it in a Barbarian, and all did forgive him,
onely this remained, that they executed their Law
notwithſtanding his repentance, and required his fine,
to which he willingly fubmitted and paid it.

Another cafe of admonition was this, *Cutſhamaquin*
the *Sachim* having a fon of about 14. or 15. yeers old,
he had bin drunk, & had behaved himfelf difobedi-
ently and rebellioufly againſt his father and mother,
for which finne they did blame him, but he defpifed
their admonition. And before I knew of it, I did
obferve when I catechized him, when he ſhould fay
the fift Commandement, he did not freely fay, *Honor
thy father*, but wholly left out *mother*, and fo he did
the Leĉture day before, but when this finne of his
was produced, he was called forth before the Affem-
G bly,

bly, and hee confeſſed that what was ſaid againſt him was true, but hee fell to accuſe his father of ſundry evils, as that hee would have killed him in his anger, and that he forced him to drink Sack, and I know not what elſe : which behavior wee greatly diſliked, ſhewed him the evill of it, and Mr. *Wilſon* being preſent laboured much with him, for hee underſtood the Engliſh, but all in vaine, his heart was hard and hopeleſſe for that time, therefore uſing due loving perſwaſions, wee did ſharply. admoniſh him of his ſinne, and required him to anſwer further the next Lecture day, and ſo left him ; and ſo ſtout he was, that when his father offered to pay his fine of 10 *s*. for his drunkenneſſe according to their Law, he would not accept it at his hand. When the next day was come, and other exerciſes finiſhed, I called him forth, and he willingly came, but ſtill in the ſame mind as before. Then wee turned to his father, and exhorted him to remove that ſtumbling block out of his ſonnes way, by confeſſing his own ſinnes whereby hee had given occaſion of hardneſſe of heart to his ſonne ; which thing was not ſuddain to him, for I had formerly in private prepared him thereunto, and hee was very willing to hearken to that counſell, becauſe his conſcience told him he was blameworthy ; and accordingly he did, he confeſſed his maine and principall evils of his own accord : and upon this advantage I took occaſion to put him upon confeſſion of ſundry other vices which I knew hee had in former times been guilty of, and all the Indians knew it likewiſe ; and put it after this manner, Are you now ſorry
for

for your drunkenneſſe, filthines, falſe dealing, lying, &c. which ſinnes you committed before you knew God? unto all which caſes, he expreſſed himſelf ſorrowfull, and condemned himſelf for them: which example of the *Sachim* was profitable for all the Indians. And when he had thus confeſſed his ſinnes, we turned againe to his ſonne and laboured with him, requiring him to confeſſe his ſinne, and intreat God to forgive him for Chriſt his ſake, and to confeſſe his offence againſt his father and mother, and intreat them to forgive him, but he ſtill refuſed; and now the other Indians ſpake unto him ſoberly, and affectionately, to put him on, and divers ſpake one after another, and ſome ſeverall times. Mr. *Wilſon* againe did much labour with him, and at laſt he did humble himſelf, confeſſed all, and intreated his father to forgive him, and took him by the hand, at which his father burſt forth into great weeping: hee did the ſame alſo to his mother, who wept alſo, and ſo did divers others; and many Engliſh being preſent, they fell a weeping, ſo that the houſe was filled with weeping on every ſide; and then we went to prayer, in all which time *Cutſhamaquin* wept in ſo much that when wee had done the board he ſtood upon was all dropped with his teares.

Another caſe of admonition was this, a hopefull young man who is my ſervant, being upon a journey, and drinking Sack at their ſetting forth, he drank too much, and was diſguiſed; which when I heard I reproved him, and he humbled himſelf, with con-feſſion of his ſinne, and teares. And the next Lecture
day

day I called him forth before the Aſſembly, where he did confeſſe his ſinne with many teares.

Before I leave this point of admonition, if I thought it would not bee too tedious to you, I would mention one particular more, where we ſaw the power of God awing a wicked wretch by this ordinance of admonition. It was *George* that wicked *Indian*, who as you know, at our firſt beginnings ſought to caſt aſperſions upon Religion, by laying ſlanderous accuſations againſt godly men, and who aſked that captious queſtion, *who made Sack?* and this fellow having kild a young Cow at your Towne, and ſold it at the Colledge inſtead of *Mooſe,* covered it with many lies, inſomuch as Mr. *Dunſter* was loath he ſhould be directly charged with it when we called him forth, but that wee ſhould rather inquire. But when he was called before the Aſſembly and charged with it, he had not power to deny it, but preſently confeſſed, onely hee added one thing which wee think an excuſe; thus God hath honored this ordinance among them.

Fourthly, the laſt exerciſe, you know, we have among them, is their aſking us queſtions, and very many they have aſked, which I have forgotten, but ſome few that have come to my preſent remembrance I will briefly touch.

One was *Wabbakomets* queſtion, who is reputed an old *Powwaw,* it was to this purpoſe, ſeeing the Engliſh had been 27 yeers (ſome of them) in this land, why did wee never teach them to know God till now? had you done it ſooner, ſaid hee, wee might have known much of God by this time, and much

ſin

fin might have been prevented, but now fome of us are grown old in fin, &c. To whom we anfwered, that we doe repent that wee did not long agoe, as how we doe, yet withall wee told them, that they were never willing to hear till now, and that feeing God hath bowed their hearts to be willing to hear, we are defirous to take all the paines we can now to teach them.

Another queftion was, that of *Cutfhamaquin,* to this purpofe, Before I knew God, faid he, I thought I was well, but fince I have known God and fin, I find my heart full of fin, and more finfull then ever it was before, and this hath been a great trouble to mee; and at this day my heart is but very little better then it was, and I am afraid it will be as bad againe as it was before, and therefore I fometime wifh I might die before I be fo bad again as I have been. Now my queftion is, whether is this a fin or not? This queftion could not be learned from the Englifh, nor did it feem a coyned feigned thing, but a reall matter gathered from the experience of his own heart, and from an inward obfervation of himfelf.

Another queftion was about their children, Whither their little children goe when they dye, feeing they have not finned?

Which queftion gave occafion more fully to teach them originall fin, and the damned ftate of all men: And alfo, and efpecially it gave occafion to teach them the Covenant of God, which he hath made with all his people, and with their children, fo that when God choofes a man or a woman to be his fer-
vant,

vant, he choofes all their children to be fo alfo:
which doctrin was exceeding gratefull unto them.

Another great queftion was this, when I preached
out of 1 *Cor.* 6. 9, 10, 11. old Mr. *Brown,* being prefent, obferved them to be much affected, and one
efpecially did weep very much, though covered it
what hee could; and after that there was a generall
queftion, which they fent unto mee about, by my
man, as the queftion of them all, *Whether any of
them fhould goe to Heaven, feeing they found their hearts
full of finne, and efpecially full of the finne of luft,* which
they call *nanwunwudfquas,* that is, mad after women;
and the next meeting, being at *Dorchefter mill,* Mr.
Mather and Mr. *Wareham,* with divers others being
prefent, they did there propound it, expreffing their
feares, *that none of them fhould bee faved;* which queftion did draw forth my heart to preach and preffe
the promife of pardon to all that were weary and fick
of finne, if they did beleeve in Chrift who had died
for us, and fatisfied the juftice of God for all our
finnes, and through whom God is well pleafed with
all fuch repenting finners that come to Chrift, and
beleeve in him; and the next day I took that Text,
Matth. 11. 28, 29. and this doctrin fome of them in
a fpeciall manner did receive in a very reverent
manner.

There is another great queftion that hath been
feverall times propounded, and much fticks with fuch
as begin to pray, namely, *If they leave off* Powwawing,
and pray to God, what fhall they do when they are fick?
for they have no fkill in phyfick, though fome of
them

them underſtand the vertues of ſundry things, yet the
ſtate of man's body, and ſkill to apply them they
have not : but all the refuge they have and rely upon
in time of ſickneſſe is their *Powwaws,* who by antick,
fooliſh and irrationall conceits delude the poore
people ; ſo that it is a very needfull thing to inform
them in the uſe of Phyſick, and a moſt effectuall
meanes to take them off from their *Powwawing.*
Some of the wiſer ſort I have ſtirred up to get this
ſkill ; I have ſhewed them the anatomy of mans body,
and ſome generall principles of Phyſick, which is
very acceptable to them, but they are ſo extreamely
ignorant, that theſe things muſt rather be taught
by ſight, ſenſe, and experience then by precepts,
and rules of art ; and therefore I have had many
thoughts in my heart, that it were a ſingular good
work, if the Lord would ſtirre up the hearts of ſome
or other of his people in England to give ſome main-
tenance toward ſome Schoole or Collegiate exerciſe
this way, wherein there ſhould be Anatomies and
other inſtructions that way, and where there might
be ſome recompence given to any that ſhould bring
in any vegetable or other thing that is vertuous in the
way of Phyſick ; by this means we ſhould ſoon have
all theſe things which they know, and others of our
Countreymen that are ſkilfull that way, and now their
ſkill lies buried for want of incouragement, would
be a ſearching and trying to find out the vertues of
things in this country, which doubtleſſe are many,
and would not a little conduce to the benefit of the
people of this Countrey, and it may bee of our native
Countrey

Countrey alſo; by this meanes wee ſhould traine up theſe poore *Indians* in that ſkill which would confound and root out their *Powwaws*, and then would they be farre more eaſily inclined to leave thoſe wayes, and pray unto God, whoſe gift Phyſick is, and whoſe bleſſing muſt make it effectuall.

There is alſo another reaſon which moves my thought and deſires this way, namely that our young Students in Phyſick may be trained up better then yet they bee, who have only theoreticall knowledge, and are forced to fall to practiſe before ever they ſaw an Anatomy made, or duely trained up in making experiments, for we never had but one Anatomy in the Countrey, which Mr. *Giles Firman* (now in England) did make and read upon very well, but no more of that now.

This very day that I wrote theſe things unto you, I have been with the *Indians* to teach them, as I was wont to doe, and one of their queſtions among many others was to know what to ſay to ſuch *Indians* as oppoſe their praying to God, and beleeving in Jeſus Chriſt, and for their own information alſo, What get you, ſay they, by praying to God, and beleeving in Jeſus Chriſt? you goe naked ſtill, and you are as poore as wee, and our Corne is as good as yours, and wee take more pleaſure then you; did we ſee that you got any thing by it, wee would pray to God and beleeve in Jeſus Chriſt alſo as you doe? Unto which queſtion I then anſwered them. Firſt, God giveth unto us two ſorts of good things, one ſort are little ones, which I ſhewed by my little finger; the other

ſort

fort are great ones, which I fhewed by my thumbe, (for you know they ufe and delight in demonftrations:) the little mercies are riches, as cloths, food, fack, houfes, cattle, and pleafures, thefe are little things which ferve but for our bodies a little while in·this life; the great mercies are wifdome, the knowledge of God, Chrift, eternall life, repentance, faith, thefe are mercies for the foule, and for eternall life: now though God do not yet give you the little mercies, he giveth you that which is a great deale better, which the wicked *Indians* cannot fee. And this I proved to them by this example; when *Foxun* the *Mohegan* Counfeller, who is counted the wifeft *Indian* in the Country, was in the *Bay*, I did on purpofe bring him unto you; and when he was here, you faw he was a foole in comparifon of you, for you could fpeak of God and Chrift, and heaven and repentance and faith, but he fate and had not one word to fay, unleffe you talked of fuch poor things as hunting, wars, &c. Secondly, you have fome more cloths then they, and the reafon why you have no more is becaufe you have but a little wifdome, if you were more wife to know God, and obey his Commands, you would work more then you do, for fo God commandeth, *Six dayes thou fhalt work,* &c. and thus the Englifh do: and if you would bee fo wife as to worke as they do, you fhould have cloths, houfes, cattle, riches as they have, God would give you them.

This day they told me this news, that fome of them having been abroad in the Country at *Titacut*, divers of thofe *Indians* would be glad to know God, and to pray unto God, and would be glad if I would come and teach them, but fome of them oppofed and

H   would

would not. They aſkt me this day, why God made
the Rainbow. Theſe things are now freſh in my
mind, that makes me ſo large in them, but I'le forbeare any more of their queſtions of this nature.

There do ſundry times fall out differences among
them, and they uſually bring their caſes to me, and
ſometime ſuch, as it's needfull for me to decline;
where I may, I adviſe them to ſome iſſue. One great
caſe that hath come ſeverall times to mee, is about
ſuch debts as they owe by gaming, for they have
been great gameſters, but have moved queſtions about
it, and are informed of the unlawfulneſſe of it, and
have thereupon wholly given over gaming for any
wagers, and all games wherein is a lot, onely uſe law-
full recreations, and have a Law againſt unlawfull
gaming; but other *Indians* that are of another mind,
come and challenge their old debts, and now they
refuſe to pay, becauſe it was a ſinne ſo to game, and
they now pray to God, and therefore muſt not pay
ſuch ſinfull debts. Now the caſe being ſerious, and
ſuch as I ſaw a ſnare underneath, the firſt counſaile
they had was, who ever would challenge ſuch a debt
ſhould come to our Governor, and he would take
order to rectifie the matter. But the Creditors liked
not that way, and therefore ſoon after there came
another caſe of the ſame kinde, an iſſue was very
neceſſary; therefore I firſt dealt with the creditor,
and ſhewed him the ſinfulneſſe of ſuch games, and
how angry God was at them; and therefore per-
ſwaded him to be content to take half his debt, unto
which he very willingly condeſcended; then I dealt
with the debtor, and aſkt him if he did not promiſe
to

to pay him all that debt? and he anfwered yea, he did fo; then I fhewed him that God commands us to performe our promifes, and though he finned in gaming, he muft repent of that, but feeing he hath promifed payment, he fhould fin to break his promife: at which he was utterly filenced; but then I afked him, if hee would willingly pay half, if I fhould perfwade the other to accept it; yea faid hee very willingly, and fo the matter ended: and in this way they ufually end fuch cafes fince that time. Their young men, who of all the reft, live moft idlely and diffolutely, now begin to goe to fervice, fome to *Indians*, fome to *Englifh*; and fome of them growing weary, broak out of their fervices, and they had no help among them for it; fo that fome propounded what they fhould doe to remedy that evill; they were anfwered, that the Englifh bring fuch fervants to the Court, and our Magiftrates rectifie thofe evills; then they defired that they might have a Court among them for government, at which motion wee rejoyced, feeing it came from themfelves, and tended fo much to civilize them, fince which time I moved the Generall Court in it, and they have pleafed to order a way for exercifing government among them: the good Lord profper and bleffe it.

They moved alfo as you know for a School, and through Gods mercy a courfe is now taken that there be Schooles at both places where their children are taught.

You know likewife that wee exhorted them to fence their ground with ditches, ftone walls, upon the banks, and promifed to helpe them with Shovels,
Spades,

Spades, Mattocks, Crows of Iron; and they are very deſirous to follow that counſell, and call upon me to help them with tooles faſter them I can get them, though I have now bought pretty ſtore, and they (I hope) are at work.   The women are deſirous to learn to ſpin, and I have procured Wheels for ſundry of them, and they can ſpin pretty well.   They begin to grow induſtrious, and find ſomething to ſell at Market all the yeer long: all winter they ſell Brooms, Staves, Elepots, Baſkets, Turkies.   In the Spring, Craneberies, Fiſh, Strawberies; in the Summer Hurtleberries, Grapes, Fiſh: in the Autumn they ſell Craneberries, Fiſh, Veniſon, &c. and they find a good benefit by the Market, and grow more and more to make uſe thereof; beſides ſundry of them work with the Engliſh in Hay time, and Harveſt, but yet it's not comparable to what they might do, if they were induſtrious, and old boughs muſt be bent a little at once; if we can ſet the young twiggs in a better bent, it will bee Gods mercy.   Deare brother I can go no further, a weary body, and ſleepy eyes command me to conclude, if I have not ſatisfied your deſire in this little I have wrote, let me underſtand it from you, and I ſhall be willing to do my indeavour: and thus with my deare love remembred to your ſelf and your beloved yoakfellow, and deſiring your prayers for Gods grace and bleſſing upon my ſpirit and poor indeavours, I take leave at this time and reſt

Roxbury this 24. of   *Your loving brother in*
   Septemb.   *our Saviour Chriſt,*
   1647.

J O H N   E L I O T.
                                              Let

Let me adde this Poftfcript, that there be two rea-
fons that make me beleeve the Lords time is come
to make a preparative at leaft for the comming of his
grace, and kingdome among them. Firft, that he
hath bowed their hearts, who were as averfe, and as
farre off from God, as any heathen in the world; and
their hearts begin to bow more and more. Secondly,
becaufe the Lord hath raifed a mighty fpirit of prayer
in this behalfe in all the Churches.

This Relation of Mr. *Eliots* I know many things
therein to be true, & all the reft I have heard con-
firmed by credible perfons, eye & eare witneffes of
thefe things, and they are familiarly known in thefe
parts. I know alfo that Mr. *Eliot* writes (as his fpirit
is) modeftly and fparingly, and fpeaks the leaft in
fundry particulars; for in his ftory of the repentance
and publike admonition of his own man, page 33.
hee faith he manifefted many teares in publike, but
I heard it from many then prefent that there were fo
many, as that the dry place of the *Wigwam* where
hee ftood was bedirtied with them, powring them
out fo abundantly. *Indians* are well known not bee
much fubject to teares, no not when they come to
feele the foreft torture, or are folemnly brought forth
to die; and if the Word workes thefe teares, furely
there is fome conquering power of Chrift Jefus ftirring among them, which what it will end in at laft,
the Lord beft knows. If Mr. *Brightmans* interpretation of *Daniels* prophefie be true, that *Anno* 1650.
Europe will hear fome of the beft tidings that ever
came into the world, *viz.* rumors from the Eafterne
Jews, which fhall trouble the Turkifh tyrant and
fhake

ſhake his Pillars when they are comming to re-
poſſeſſe their own land, for which they will be
wraſtling (if my memory failes not, according to
his notion) about 40. yeers; I ſhall hope then
that theſe Weſterne *Indians* will ſoon come in,
and that theſe beginnings are but preparatives for a
brighter day then we yet ſee among them, wherein
Eaſt & Weſt ſhall ſing the ſong of the Lambe: but
I have no ſkill in propheſies, nor do I beleeve every
mans interpretation of ſuch Scripture; but this is
certain, God is at work among theſe; and it is not
uſual for the Sun to ſet as ſoon as it begins to riſe,
nor for he Lord to Jeſus to loſe an inch of ground in
the recovering times of his Churches peace and his
own eclipſed and forgotten glory, (if theſe bee ſuch
times) untill hee hath won the whole field, and driven
the Prince of darkneſſe out of it, who is but a bold
uſurper of ·the Lord Jeſus inheritance, to whom are
given the utmoſt ends of the earth.   When *Charles*
the Great had broken the chief power of the barba-
rous and fierce *Saxons* in *Germany*, he made this the
onely article of peace, that they ſhould entertain ſuch
a Goſpel as good then as the degenerate Chriſtian
world could affoord, and for that end admit of a Monaſtery among them of ſuch men as might inſtruct
them, and this courſe prevailed, if wee may beleeve *Crantzius the Hiſtorian of thoſe times; and
ſhall wee think that when the Lord Jeſus hath
ſet up not a Monaſtery of workes but Churches of
Saints in theſe coaſts to encourage the miniſtry and
this work of Chriſt, that his bleſſed Goſpel cannot or
ſhall not in theſe dayes take ſome effect ſince it hath
broke ſo far?   I dare conclude nothing, onely it will
be

*Crantzius
lib. 1. cb. 1, 2.*

be our comfort in the day of our accounts, that wee have endeavored fomething this way; and it may be this very indeavour fhall be our peace. *Gildas* our Britifh Hiftorian obferving that one caufe why God let loofe the *Saxons* to fcourge and root out the *Britaines,* was their deep careleffneffe of communicating unto them the Chriftian Religion, when they had their fpirits at fit advantage: but I dare not difcourfe of thefe matters.

One thing more I remember concerning Mr. *Eliots* conference with a *Narraganfet Sachim* a fober man this yeer; after that he had taught this *Sachim* the Law of God, and had fhewen him the means of falvation by Chrift; he then afked him if he did not know and underftand thofe things? and he faid, yes. He then afked him if he did beleeve them? but hee could not get anfwer from him that way, but did feeme to take them into more ferious thoughts. He then afked him, why they did not learn of Mr. *Williams* who hath lived among them divers yeers? and he foberly anfwered that they did not care to learn of him, becaufe hee is no good man but goes out and workes upon the Sabbath day; I name it not to fhew what glimmerings nature may have concerning the obfervation of the Sabbath, but to fhew what the ill example of Englifh may doe, and to fee what a ftumbling block to all Religion the loofe obfervation of the Sabbath is, however mans fhifting wits may find out evafions, to get loofe from out of that net.

But this may ferve to fatisfie your own or others defires concerning the progreffe of the Gofpel among the *Indians :* the Lord Jefus feemes at this day to bee
turning

turning upſide down the whole frame of things in
the world, Kings, Parliaments, Armies, Kingdomes,
Authorities, Churches, Miniſters, and if out of his
free grace hee looks not upon theſe hopefull beginnings, theſe will be ſo turned alſo ; for oppoſition
there is from men and devils againſt it, and I have
feared in my own heart that within theſe few moneths
there hath been ſome coolings among the beſt of
theſe *Indians;* but wee find it ſo alſo among many
people that are *Engliſh* in their firſt work, but the
Lord Jeſus revives again ; and therefore Mr. *Eliot* of
late having told them that hee was afraid that they
began to bee weary, they took it to heart, and propounded in my hearing at a late *Indian* Lecture at
Noonanetum many profitable queſtions, viz. *When they
prayed and heard the Word aright ? and how they might
know when they were weary of them ? And what time it
might bee before the Lord might come and make them
know him ? And what the firſt ſinne of the Devils was ?*
(Hee diſcourſing to them about the danger of Apoſ-
taſie.)   At this time they are (as you may perceive
by Mr. *Eliots* writings) about fencing in their ground
and Town given them ſome hundreds of Acres, with
a ſtone fence, for which end Mr. *Eliot* provides them
Mattocks, Shovels and Crowes of Iron, &c. and to
encourage their ſlothfulneſſe, promiſed to give a
groat or ſix pence a rod, if they would thus farre
attend their own good, and work for themſelves : all
the poor *Indians* at *Noonanetum* are generally clad with
ſuch cloths as wee can get them, and the *Wigwams*
of the meaneſt of them equallize any *Sachims* in other
places, being built not with mats but barks of Trees

in

in good bigneſſe, the rather that they may have their partitions in them for huſbands and wives togeather, and their children and ſervants in their places alſo, who formerly were never private in what nature is aſhamed of, either for the ſun or any man to ſee. It's ſome refreſhing to thinke that there is (if there was no more but) the name of Chriſt ſounding in thoſe darke and deſpicable *Tartarian* Tents; the Lord can build them houſes in time to pray in, when hee hath given unto them better hearts, and when perhaps hee hath curſed and conſumed theirs who have diſdained to give that worſhip and homage to Chriſt in their ſeiled houſes, which poor *Indians* rejoyce to give to him in their poor Tents and *Wigwams :* I deſire you to gather what ſtock of prayers you can for them. I had almoſt forgot to tell you of Mr. *Eliots* going up the Country lately with Mr. *Flint,* Captain *Willard* of *Concord,* and ſundry others, towards *Merrimath* River unto that *Indian Sachim Paſſaconnaway,* that old Witch and *Powwaw,* who together with both his ſons, fled the preſence of the light, and durſt not ſtand their ground, nor be at home when he came, pretending feare of being killed by a man forſooth that came only with a book in his hand, and with a few others without any weapons only to bear him company and direct his way in thoſe deſerts; but in it you may ſee the guilt of the man, & that *Satan* is but a coward in his *Lyons* ſkin even upon his own dunghill, as alſo the hatred and enmity againſt the Word which is in ſome, which argues that the attention which others give to it, is a power of God, and

I   not

not meerly to flatter and get favour with the Englifh :
but the reft of *Paffaconnawaies* men attended to the
things which were fpoken and afked divers queftions,
the *Indians* in our parts accompanying Mr. *Eliot* and
giving bleffed examples to the others herein, as alfo
in faying Grace before and after meat, praying in
their *Wigwams* with them, and fome of them fing-
ing of Pfalmes, which they have learnt among the
Englifh : difcourfing alfo with them about the things
of God.   It is fomewhat obfervable (though the obfervation bee more cheerfull than deep) that the firft
Text out of which Mr. *Eliot* preached to the *Indians*
was about the dry bones, *Ezek.* 37. where it's faid,
Verf. 9, 10. *that by prophefying to the wind, the wind
came and the dry bones lived;* now the *Indian* word
for Wind is *Waubon,* and the moft active *Indian* for
ftirring up other *Indians* to feek after the knowledg
of God in thefe parts, his name is *Waubon,* which
fignifies Wind, (the *Indians* giving names to their
children ufually according to appearances of providences) although they never dreamt of this, that
this their *Waubon* fhould breathe fuch a fpirit of
life and incouragement into the reft of the *Indians,*
as hee hath indeavored in all parts of the Countrey,
both at *Concord, Merrimeck* and elfewhere ; but
fome of the *Indians* themfelves that were ftir'd up by
him took notice of this his name and that Scripture
together, and the Englifh alfo have much obferved
him herein, who ftill continues the fame man,
although we thinke there be now many others whom
he firft breathed encouragement into that do farre
                                                    exceed

exceed him in the light and life of the things of God : Mr. *Eliot* alſo profeſſing that he choſe that Text without the leaſt thought of any ſuch application in reſpeсt of *Waubon.*

There have been many difficult queſtions pro-pounded by them, which we have been unwilling to engage our ſelves in any anſwer unto, untill wee have the concurrence of others with us.

Firſt, ſuppoſe a man before hee knew God, hath had two wives, the firſt barren and childleſſe, the ſecond fruitfull and bearing him many ſweet children, the queſtion now propounded was, *Which of theſe two wives he is to put away ?* if hee puts away ; the firſt who hath no children, then hee puts away her whom God and Religion undoubtedly binds him unto, there being no other defeсt but want of children : if hee puts away the other, then he muſt caſt off all his children with her alſo as illegitimate, whom hee ſo exceedingly loves. This is a caſe now among them, and they are very fearefull to do any thing croſſe to Gods will and mind herein.

Secondly, ſuppoſe a man marry a *Sqaw,* and ſhee deſerts and flies from her huſband, and commits adultery with other remote *Indians,* but afterward it come to paſſe that ſhee hearing the Word, and ſorry for what ſhee hath done, ſhe deſires to come to her huſband againe, who remaines ſtill unmarried ; *Whe-ther ſhould this huſband upon her repentance receive her againe ? and whether is he not bound thereunto ſo to doe ?*

At the laſt Leсture at *Noonanetum* this *September,* there were divers queſtions aſked : one was pro-pounded

pounded by an old *Sqaw*, a Widow; viz. *If when
men know God, God loves them, why then is it that any
one are afflicted after that they know him?* I ſhall
mention no more, but conclude with the ſolemn
ſpeech of a ſober and hopefull *Indian* at this Lecture,
whoſe name is *Wampooas*, who in ſtead of propounding a queſtion fell into theſe expreſſions, viz. " That
" becauſe wee pray to God, other *Indians* abroad in
" the countrey hate us and oppoſe us, the Engliſh on
" the other ſide ſuſpect us, and feare us to be ſtill ſuch
" as doe not pray at all; but (ſaith he) God who
" knowes all things, he knowes that wee do pray to
" him. To which ſpeech Mr. *Eliot* replyed, that it
was true indeed, that ſome of the Engliſh did ſo far
ſuſpect them for ſundry reaſons; but I doe not ſo,
and others of us, who know you and ſpeake with you,
we do not ſo think of you; and then gave them gracious and ſerious incouragements to goe forward and
make more progreſſe in the things of God. This
their own teſtimony of themſelves being propounded
with much ſweetneſſe and ſeriouſneſſe of affection,
may be the laſt, although it be the leaſt confirmation
of ſome inward worke among them; which I looked
upon as a ſpeciall providence that ſuch a ſpeech ſhould
be ſpoken and come to my eare juſt at ſuch a time as
this, wherein I was finiſhing the ſtory, to confirme
in ſome meaſure what hath been written; the Lord
himſelf I beleeve and no man living, putting theſe
words into their own hearts, to give this modeſt teſtimony concerning themſelves. The beginning of
this enlargement of Chriſts Kingdome ſhould inlarge
our

our hearts with great joy. If I fhould gather and fumme up together the feverall gracious impreffions of God upon them from what hath been fcattered here and there in the ftory, I thinke 'it might make many Chriftians afhamed, who may eafily fee how farre they are exceeded by thefe naked men in fo fhort a time thus wrought upon by fuch fmall and defpicable means.   My brother *Eliot* who is Preacher to them, profeffing he can as yet but ftammer out fome peeces of the Word of God unto them in their own tongue; but God is with him, and God is wont to be *maximus in minimis*, and is moft feene in doing great things by fmall meanes.   The Sword of Gods Word fhall and will pierce deep, even when it is half broken, when the hand of a mighty Redeemer hath the laying of it on : and the Scripture herein is, and muft be fulfilled, that as foon as the heathen heare Chrift they fhall fubmit, *Pfal.* 18. 43, 44. and fuch nations whom Chrift knew not fhall run unto him, *Ifai.* 55. 5. The fall of the unbeleving Jewes was the rifing of the Gentiles; my prayer to God therefore for *Europe* is, that the fall of the Churches, (little bettered by the devouring Sword which is ftill thirfty) may not bee the rifing of thefe *American* Gentiles, never pitied till now.   I wifh that *Alftedius* prophefie herein may never prove true; but rather that the rifing of thefe may be a provoking and raifing up of them, efpe-cially of the Englifh, to lament after that God whom they have forfaken; and to lament after him, together with us, for thefe poor *Indians* who never yet knew him.

Sir,

Sir, I had ended theſe relations once or twice, but the ſtay of the Veſſell increaſeth new matter; which becauſe 'tis new and freſh, you ſhall have it as I heard of it from a faithfull hand : There were ſundry queſtions propounded at the *Indian* Lecture at *Noonanetum* this *Octob.* 13. by the *Indians:* the firſt was propounded to Mr. *Eliot* himſelf upon occaſion of his Sermon out *Epheſ.* 5. 11. *Have no fellowſhip with unfruitfull workers of darknes,* viz. *What Engliſh men did thinke of* Mr. Eliot *becauſe he came among wicked Indians to teach them?*

Secondly, *Suppoſe two men ſinne, the one knowes he ſinneth, and the other doth not know ſinne, will God puniſh both alike?*

Thirdly, *Suppoſe there ſhould be one wiſe Indian that teacheth good things to other Indians, whether ſhould not he be as a father or brother unto ſuch Indians he ſo teacheth in the wayes of God?* This laſt queſtion ſeemes to argue ſome motions ſtirring in ſome of their hearts to pity and teach their poor Countreymen; and ſurely then will bee the moſt hopefull time of doing good among them, when the Lord ſhall raiſe up ſome or other like themſelves to go among them and preach the Word of life unto them with fatherly or brotherly bowels; and yet I limit not the moſt High, who can make uſe of what Inſtruments hee pleaſeth for this work. I ſhall conclude therefore with a ſtory I had both by writing and word of mouth, from a faithfull *man which hee ſaw with his own eyes this *Octob.* 7. There was one of the *Indians* at *Noonanetum*, hath had a child ſick

Mr. Edward Iackſon.

of

of a Confumption many a day, and at that time died
of it ; when it was dead, fome of the *Indians* came to
an honeft man to enquire how they fhould bury their
dead ; the man told them how and what the Englifh
did when they buried theirs; hereupon rejecting all
their old fuperftitious obfervances at fuch fad times
(which are not a few) they prefently procured a few
boards, and buy a few nayles of the *Englifh*, and fo
make a pretty handfome Coffin, (for they are very
dextrous at any thing they fee once done) and put
the child into it, and fo accompanied it to the grave
very folemnly, about 40. *Indians* of them : when the
earth was caft upon it and the grave made up, they
withdrew a little from that place, and went all together and affembled under a Tree in the Woods,
and there they defired one *Tutafwampe* a very hopefull *Indian* to pray with them; now although the
Englifh do not ufually meet in companies to pray together after fuch fad occafions, yet it feemes God ftird
up their hearts thus to doe ; what the fubftance of
their prayer was I cannot certainly learn, although I
I have heard fome things that way, which I therefore name not, onely I have and fhall indeavour
to get it, if it bee poffible for the poor *Indian* to
expreffe the fubftance of it, and fo fhall fend it if
the fhip ftayes long, onely this is certaine by him
who was occafionally an eye and eare witneffe of
thefe things, that they continued inftant with God
in prayer for almoft half an houre together, and this
godly mans words to mee (who underftands a little
of their language) are thefe; that this *Tutafwampe*
did

did expreſſe ſuch zeale in prayer with ſuch variety
of gracious expreſſions, and abundance of teares,
both of himſelf and moſt of the company, that
the woods rang againe with their ſighes and prayers;
and (ſaith he) I was much aſhamed of my ſelf and
ſome others, that have had ſo great light, and yet
want ſuch affections as they have, who have as yet ſo
little knowledge. All this he ſaw ſtanding at ſome
good diſtance alone from them under a Tree.

Thus you ſee (Sir) that theſe old obdurate ſinners
are not altogether ſenſeleſſe of Gods afflicting hand
and humbling providences; and though naturall
affection may be much ſtirring in ſuch times, yet you
ſee how God begins to ſanctifie ſuch affections among
them : and I wiſh that many Engliſh were not out-
ſtript herein by theſe poor *Indians,* who have got the
ſtart I feare of many *Engliſh,* that can paſſe by ſuch
ſad providences without laying them in this manner
to heart. I confeſſe theſe and many ſuch things
which wee ſee in divers of them, do make ſome to
thinke that there is more of God and his Spirit in
ſome of their hearts then we yet can diſcover, and
which they hope will break out in time.

Thus you have a true, but ſomewhat rent and ragged relation of theſe things; it may be moſt ſutable
to the ſtory of naked and ragged men : my deſire is
that no mans Spectacles may deceive him, ſo as to
look upon theſe things either as bigger or leſſer, better or worſer then they are; which all men generally
are apt to doe at things at ſo great diſtance, but that
they may judge of them as indeed they are, by what
                                                    truth

truth they fee here expreft in the things themfelves. I know that fome thinke that all this worke among them is done and acted thus by the *Indians* to pleafe the *Englifh*, and for applaufe from them; and it is not unlikely but fo 'tis in many, who doe but blaze for a time; but certainly 'tis not fo in all, but that the power of the Word hath taken place in fome, and that inwardly and effectually, but how far fav-ingly time will declare, and the reader may judge of, by the ftory it felf of thefe things. Some fay that if it be fo, yet they are but a few that are thus wrought upon; Be it fo, yet fo it hath ever been, *many called, few chofen:* and yet withall I beleeve the calling in of a few *Indians* to Chrift is the gathering home of many hundreds in one, confidering what a vaft dif-tance there hath been between God and them fo long, even dayes without number; confidering alfo how pre-cious the firft fruits of *America* will be to Jefus Chrift, and what feeds they may be of great harvefts in after times; and yet if there was no great matter feen in thefe of grown yeers, their children notwithftanding are of great hopes both from *Englifh* and *Indians* themfelves, who are therefore trained up to Schoole, where many are very apt to learne, and who are alfo able readily to anfwer to the queftions propounded, containing the principles and grounds of all Chriftian Religion in their own tongue. I confeffe it paffeth my fkill to tell how the Gofpel fhould be generally received by thefe *American* Natives, confidering the variety of Languages in fmall diftances of places; onely hee that made their eares and tongues can raife

K up

up some or other to teach them how to heare, and what to spake; and if the Gospel muſt ride circuit, Chriſt can and will conquer by weake and deſpicable meanes, though the conqueſt perhaps may be ſomewhat long.   The beginnings and foundations of the *Spaniard* in the Southerne parts of this vaſt continent, being laid in the blood of nineteene Millions of poor innocent Natives (as *Acoſta* the Jeſuite a bird of their own neſt relates the ſtory) ſhall certainly therefore bee utterly rooted up by ſome revenging hand; and when he is once diſpoſſeſt of his Golden Manſions and Silver Mines, it may be then the oppreſſed remnant in thoſe coaſts alſo may come in.   In the meane while if it bee the good pleaſure of Chriſt to look upon any of the worſt and meaneſt of theſe outcaſts in theſe Coaſts of *New-England,* let us not deſpiſe this day of ſmall things, but as the Jews did of old, ſo let us now cry mightily to God and ſay, and ſing, *Let the people praiſe thee O God, yea let all the people praiſe thee, then ſhall the earth bring forth her increaſe, and God even our God will bleſſe us.*

*I have ſent you two witneſſes beſide my own
    of the truth of the Indian ſtory printed,
    you may publiſh them if you pleaſe as they
    have writ, and ſubſcrib'd with their own
    hands.*

                        THOMAS SHEPHARD.

F I N I S.

www.ingramcontent.com/pod-product-compliance
Lightning Source LLC
Chambersburg PA
CBHW022145090426
42742CB00010B/1397